POPULATION PRIMER

by

FRANCES FRECH

CARTOONS BY DICK HAFER

Anastasia Books

Washington • Stafford

I.S.B.N. No. 0-913631-00-0

Anastasia Books is a publication division of
American Life Education and Research Trust,
a non-profit educational institution.

American Life
Education and Research Trust
P.O. Box 279
Stafford, Virginia 22554
(703) 690-2049

To my youngest son, Troy,
who encouraged the writing
of this book with his question,
"How many words did you write today?"

Frances Frech
And Dick Hafer

The Author

Frances Frech has a degree in history from the University of Kansas. She has published many articles on population and related subjects, and has presented papers at three United Nations world conferences (World Population, Bucharest, 1974; International Women's Year, Mexico City, 1975; and Habitat, Vancouver, 1976).

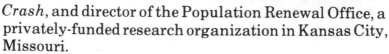

She has been a frequent guest lecturer in high schools and colleges, and has appeared on dozens of radio and TV talk shows, including NBC-TV's Today Show.

She is the author of *The Great American Stork Market Crash*, and director of the Population Renewal Office, a privately-funded research organization in Kansas City, Missouri.

The Illustrator

Dick Hafer has an extensive career in commercial art as art director for a major retail firm (Co-op Stores), a major industrial firm (Rental Tools and Equipment)

THE STORY OF THE
COMICS COMMANDO

THERE'S A MASTER COMMANDO HERE TO SEE YOU SIR

and a prominent D.C.-area advertising firm. He is the winner of numerous awards including ones from the National Press Association and the Freedom Foundation for cartooning. He has achieved national recognition for cartoon books he prepared for Joseph Sugarman & Associates, Citizens Organized to Replace Kennedy, and NCPAC. Mr. Hafer has an active background in the Lutheran Church, Missouri Synod, and is an elder in a large Washington-area Baptist congregation.

Table of Contents

Introduction

Clarence Cook is 90 years old. He makes appearances as guest history lecturer in Chicago schools as part of a federally-funded project called Living History. He amazes youngsters in junior high classes with his memories of the way it was in his own childhood.

No paved roads on Chicago's West Side. Wooden sidewalks. Hikes of a mile each way to attend a one-room school. No running water, just a big pail with a dipper in it. No peanut butter for his jelly sandwiches—it hadn't been developed yet. No radio, no TV, no video games. No electricity. No refrigeration. His family put food in a wooden box on the back porch in winter, bought blocks of ice in summer.

Contrasting all that with what people have today and take for granted, Mr. Cook comments, "I grew up in the fastest century there's ever been."

Billy Reynolds, a 12-year-old listening to one of the lectures, thought he would have preferred living at the turn of the century.

"You didn't have that much to worry about," he explained, "No inflation, no overpopulation, things like that."

Overpopulation? A 12-year-old kid is concerned about overpopulation? The time has come to teach some proper facts on the subject! That's why I decided, as a population analyst and writer, to do this Population Primer. Some of it may be too complex for a boy as young as Billy, but I'm addressing it to him, anyhow, in the hope that he'll understand and enjoy much of it.

The rest of it will be useful for high school students, and even for those in college—if they are willing to consider the possibility that what they've been taught over the years may not be true.

Frances Frech

Chapter One.
Population Games

Billy, let's play some games. As you probably know, the basic idea of the "zero population growth" movement is that everything would be just great if nobody had more than two children (well, maybe not great, but better than it is). Its promoters even think that the population would stay at its present size, neither growing **nor declining**, if the two-child family were the only kind around.

So let's find out what might really happen if no one had more than two children, if in fact no one had **ever** had more than that. We will need a group of people—any number. You can try it out on a class at school, a scout meeting, a gathering of friends on the library steps, a party. Just for fun we'll play it like "Simon Says."

Simon says everybody stand up. Simon says, if you are a third or later child in your family, sit down. Simon says, if either of your biological parents is a third or later child, sit down (if either or both of them hadn't been born, neither would you). Simon says, if any one of your grandparents was a third or later child, sit down. And if you don't know the birth order of your grandparents or parents, sit down, because you can't say for sure that they would have been born.

See how quickly the population disappears? There may be a few left standing in the third round, but if we continued the game, they would be gone, too, sooner or later.

What's that, Billy? You say the game proves how fast the population grows if there's a third child. No, it doesn't. Remember that Simon says "a third or **later** child." Many people in the group were fourth or fifth or more. I want you to remember, too, that the disappearance of the players was not due to war, famine, disease or natural disasters. It came about only because third or later children were not born.

How about a little game of Population Chess? Think about the world being a giant chess board, with people as chess pieces to be moved around by those who have the power. Leaders of population control groups would like to give such power to governments. I'm sure it would be great fun for them, but not so much fun for the chess pieces.

At the World Population Conference in Bucharest in 1974, I heard a young American Indian girl speak, and what she had to say impressed me deeply.

"Do you know what turned me off on population control?" she said. "It was the very sound of it. Population control—it sounds like rat control. Pest control. Disease control. But population— that's **people**. They're talking about people whose lives they'll play with like chess pieces."

Then there's the popular game Pin the Tail on the Donkey. Some population-control-minded people ran a two-page ad in the *New York Times*. One page had a

picture of a cute little baby. The other page was headlined "Before we can lick population, we have to do something about this little fellow." Pin the tail on the donkey, pin the blame on the baby. But the new infant pollutes far less than anybody else does. It's when he grows up and starts driving a car, needing a job, a house of his own, furniture, appliances and all that, that's when he may become a strain on the environment. If we aren't going to do anything about pollution before today's babies grow up, we might as well forget it. Incidentally, the *Times* ad was signed by a number of wealthy industrialists who do their share of polluting.

We could play Motherhood Monopoly. In that game every time a family has a new baby, they lose a new car, a color TV or a vacation. The child is reduced to less value than material possessions or moments of pleasure.

Yes, Billy? You've heard that it costs about $150,000 these days to have a baby and bring him up to the age of 18?

Some say that. Other estimates range from $100,000 to $130,000 or so. But the figures are distorted in many ways. For example, we're told that the medical expense of having a baby is around $2,000 and rising. But most people have medical insurance to take care of a large part of the cost, while the baby's fair share of the premiums would be relatively small. For those who don't, there are clinics with lower costs. And for those on welfare, there's Medicaid.

In the estimates of child-rearing expenses housing is included. But the parents have to live somewhere, and it's usually unfair to pro-rate a full share for the child. Utility bills are included, but a child adds little to these. And once again, the parents would have to use heat, lights, water and the telephone, in any case. Transportation expenses are listed, but unless these are directly related to having to take the child somewhere—music lessons, meetings—it's unfair to assess them. The child is going to travel with the parents, generally.

Some estimates include the mother's lost wages for the whole 18 years! But if she plans to work, she usually does so by the time the child is in school, at five or six years of age. If she works before that, of course, she has child care expenses, but she can get a tax credit for some of these.

And I've never seen a child-cost estimate that included the child tax-benefit. Yet a child ordinarily is a tax dependent for 19 years (longer if a full-time student), and the current amount of the exemption is $1,000 per year (parents save the amount of the tax they would have paid on the money). Additionally, low-income families with children can receive "earned income credit," a kind of reverse income tax giving them a refund even if they pay no taxes.

Children might also increase the family's income by providing the parents with greater incentives to

work. Some teenagers earn a considerable amount of money on their own, as well.

There are other games we could play—Doubling-Time Dominoes, Compound-Interest Caper, and more— but for now, let's move on to whatever you need to know about population. Ready, Billy? Just don't forget what Simon says about that two-child family plan!

Chapter Two.
Making Room

I've seen a Planned Parenthood slogan that says, "No population problem? How dense can you get?"

Let's consider density, then, although it's not too significant as a measure of a nation's ability to support its people. Some of the most densely-populated countries in the world have better living standards than many others that are sparsely settled. Where would you rather live, in the Netherlands which has over 1,000 people per square mile, or the Sahel, in Africa, with only one or two?

If the United States had a billion people—a figure that's highly unlikely given our present birth rate—our population density would be around 250 persons per square mile. Sounds horrible? Well, as Fred Domville put it in his excellent testimony before the President's Commission on Population Growth and America's Future, "If you've been to Ohio, you've already seen it" (that kind of density).

We could put the entire population of our country into the **front seats** of our cars and trucks. So perhaps that's what we have too many of—motor vehicles. The automobile is a large factor in solid waste pollution— abandoned cars in woods, in ravines, on roadsides, in junkyards. Over 100 million nearly indestructible tires

are thrown away every year. The car is a major factor in the depletion of resources, especially petroleum and metals (although, of course, the latter can be recycled). It contributes heavily to air pollution. It requires that large amounts of good land be paved over for highways and parking lots.

The late Dr. Thomas Jermann, who taught history at Rockhurst College in Kansas City, once proposed that we should have "zero automobile growth." He suggested the following measures to achieve it:

(a) A congressional resolution declaring the one-car family to be the American ideal;

(b) Higher tax rates for the second car, still higher for the third;

(c) Tolls on cars entering cities. No charge for vehicles with five or more passengers. A small charge for those with three or four, a large one for the two-passenger car and a huge one for the car with only one person in it.

Cars take up more space than people do. Ten thousand persons walking to work in the morning would make a good-sized crowd. But riding in cars (especially singly), they need six to eight times more room, bumper-to-bumper.

What did you say, Billy? This is a small planet and we can't make it bigger?

But we **can**, and we've done it. Not larger in total area, of course, but in other ways. When human beings learned to build houses of more than one story, they lifted the living space off the ground and made the earth bigger. Apartment buildings rising hundreds of feet high have made the earth bigger.

Learning how to farm and to produce more food from less land has made the earth bigger. Improvement in the breeding of food animals and breakthroughs in the storing and preserving of foods have made the capacity of the earth to feed us grow.

"Making the earth bigger" is not only possible but is being done. There's room enough and resources enough for all who are here and all who may come in the foreseeable future. Some people talk of colonizing other planets, through the development of useful space travel, as a way of "making room."

That's not likely to be necessary—ever—but there's another reason for considering such plans. Poets and science fiction writers say that man can survive as a species only so long as the sun keeps shining. And they're right, as dreamers and visionaries often are, because the sun by itself is not constant in its size and heat. Some projections say the sun will engulf the earth in the distant future; others say the sun is dying and that the earth will eventually die. Unless we can go into the reaches of space and establish colonies on new

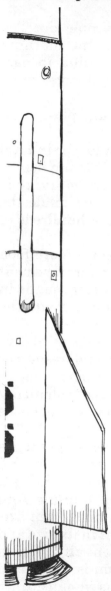

planets, the human race and its physical home may someday simply cease to be. Ray Bradbury in his short story "The Strawberry Window" explains the concept in a compelling way. If you haven't read it, look it up. You'll find it in more than one of his collections of short stories. I read it in the one called *The Day It Rained Forever*, Granada Publishing, 1977.

Without continued population growth, however, man will never reach the stars. Declining populations growing old will have neither the desire nor the ability to do it. But even maintaining our present life on earth can be difficult. For there are always either "too many" or "too few." The "too many" could be motivated to move forward, if they aren't cut down; the "too few" could die out before their time.

For so many reasons the world's children are desperately needed. "A little child will lead them" is as true in the human

OH, THE HECK WITH IT!

sense as it is in the religious one. It has always been "for the children" that men and women have striven for a better world. It is because of their families, the needs of their children, that people have taken part in trying to build a just and secure society. Without children there is no interest in the future.

"How dense can you get?" It's a meaningless question to ask in the United States. With an average family size of 1.8, expected by many students of population trends to fall to 1.5 before the end of the century, we're in a **decline cycle**. We're not yet declining in sheer numbers, but we're headed that way.

Clarence Cook, whose story I told you at the beginning of this book, says he grew up in the "fastest century." There were about 63 million people here when he was born; there were about 226 million in 1980. Charles Westoff, former executive director of the Commission on Population Growth, predicts that our population will reach 250 million 50 years from now but will decline thereafter. Mr. Cook was born just before the turn of the 20th century; a child born at the turn of the 21st is likely to grow up in the "fastest century going down."

"How dense can you get?" The question has two meanings. The second one was intended to apply to those who aren't worried about population growth. It can also be used to label those who believe that a declining population can survive when its fall is caused by its failure to have children—to have **enough** children to maintain a proper balance of young and old.

Chapter Three.
People and Pollution

Many people are especially concerned about pollution of the environment. They see reducing population as the solution to the problem. Some even go so far as to say that people are pollution. In my first book, *The Great American Stork Market Crash*, I responded to that challenge:

In the first place, people are not pollution any more than birds or animals or fish are pollution. The waste products of human bodies are no more polluting than are the waste products of other living creatures. We flush our waste products into the water; the waste products of other species often also go into the water, washed there by rainfall and runoffs. But this kind of waste is easily treated.

Man pollutes more than the animals do because of the way he lives. Part of the problem isn't his own fault. He was born naked—no fur coat or feathers to keep him warm. So he had to have clothing, which meant that, from time to time, he had something to discard. He needed shelter from the wind and rain. Caves weren't too satisfactory, though he did live in them. But living in a cave is restrictive, and to provide more living space, man had to build his own shelter, increasing the pile of discards as the shelter deteriorated or was abandoned.

Man developed a preference for cooked food, and his cook fires put polluting smoke into the air. He was born without natural weapons—no claws or fangs. So he had to make weapons, and these were added to the solid-waste piles eventually. But, of course, none of these things were really serious problems until man became more and more civilized, and wanted more and more possessions.

He learned to write down his thoughts to share them with others. At first he used rocks or tree barks, and these didn't affect the environment. But as he grew in mind and inventive powers, he manufactured paper, ink, printing presses, newspapers and books. These all added to pollution problems, first, because of the process of manufacturing and, second, because of the difficulty in discarding outmoded products.

He was restless and didn't want to stay where he was born. He couldn't go far enough on his own two legs, so he used animals to transport him. Then he made boats; and he invented the wheel and made carts and chariots. Eventually came the automobile and the airplane in increasing numbers, which posed more serious forms of pollution, especially air pollution.

He established cities for mutual benefits and protection. Because solid buildings couldn't be rolled up like the tents of Indians, he couldn't move on when the surrounding area became too dirty to live in. The Indian tribes could go somewhere else, and what they left behind eventually eroded or decayed and went back into the soil. Civilized man had to find a way to remove the solid waste from around him. He had to have garbage-disposal systems and junkyards.

His early weapons—the stone hammers and such—didn't damage his environment. The later ones, the bombs, the gunpowder and the poison gases, did.

What I'm trying to say is that people, **per se**, are not pollution; it is the way they live that creates the problems. But such problems do have solutions.

What are the solutions? Once again, I'll quote from my first book:

Water pollution is mainly the result of industrial waste. The enforcement of anti-pollution laws, many of which existed even in the 1800s, would improve the situation immensely. If it became enormously expensive, because of the fines levied against them, for industries to pour their waste material into the water, they would cease doing so.

Chemicals can be reclaimed, reused or sold for a profit. Many factories are doing just that—making money from chemicals they used to dump into the water.

Air-pollution problems can be lessened by enforcing the laws requiring factories to install antipollution devices. In fact, the air in most cities is already cleaner than it was five years ago—and according to the Environmental Protection Agency, it wasn't as dirty as everyone thought in the first place.

Much of our urban air pollution comes from the automobile. We should work to minimize the problem by controlling the use of the car. Cutting the birth rate won't help—the potential drivers for the next 17 or 18 years have already been born. We need to establish mass-transit systems and encourage people to ride them. Perhaps we should discourage the use of the automobile, even by prohibiting it altogether in certain parts of the cities.

Solid-waste pollution can be solved in many ways: Reclaiming and recycling of material; burning some of it for power; using it to fill in strip mines.

There are other pollution solutions. One company has discovered a way to grind up discarded tires to make paving materials. Glass can be ground to make building material. Solid waste can be burned in special incinerators to produce energy (many European cities have done this for years, and some cities and towns in the United States are now trying it).

Cleaning up messes often costs a great deal of

money. A reduced population, with a smaller tax base, would have a harder time providing the money. The clean-up also takes labor—the labor of young people capable of doing it.

My generation may have contributed a lot to the problem, but please don't ask **me** to do the necessary work to correct it. I haven't got the strength. One young lady at one of my lectures asked me why **she** should clean it up if I made the mess. I told her, "Because I can't do it. I'm too old. So you only have two choices: Live in the dirt, or do something about it."

Pollution, of course, isn't a new problem. Every generation has left some accumulation behind for the next group to take care of in some way. It's part of inter-generational life.

Chapter Four.
Population and
Food Supplies

Fear of going hungry seems to underlie much of the fear of population growth. The real problem is not lack of available food but lack of money to buy it. The poor in any nation are the ones who are hungry. Yet there are population control leaders such as Dr. Garrett Hardin and the late Dr. Philip Handler (of the National Academy of Sciences), who have insisted that we shouldn't feed them because if we do, they'll only have children and compound the problem.

It's simple-minded to say that hunger is caused by too many people and too little food. It can also be caused in part by too many people eating too much food and leaving too little for others. It can be caused by

WHAT A SHAME!
THERE ISN'T ENOUGH FOOD TO GO AROUND FOR THE POOR FOLKS.

wasteage. Some experts say that 50 percent of the food produced in the world is eaten by rats, insects or birds, or rots in fields because of the lack of storage facilities, or spoils because of lack of knowledge about preservation.

Those who say there would be more food if there were fewer people have overlooked the fact that cultivated food crops do not plant themselves. They do not harvest themselves, nor take themselves to the processing plants or the market place. They do not package themselves or place themselves on supermarket shelves. It takes people to do all these necessary tasks. In modern life with fewer people there could actually be less food.

According to the United Nations Food and Agriculture Organization in Rome, the world produces **every year** twice as much food in cereal grains **alone** as is needed by the total population. And four times that much could be produced with existing technology. That's **eight** times as much (twice times four) as is needed.

Undeniably, there is hunger—too much hunger—in the world. It occurs now, and occurred even when populations were smaller. People starve in Cambodia and were starving in Biafra because of war. People starved in Ireland one and a half centuries ago because the potato crop failed. Those nations which had more than enough food either couldn't or wouldn't deliver it to the Irish. People starved in America at Donner Pass because they tried to cross it at the wrong time of the year and were trapped by snow. Washington's army starved at Valley Forge. People starved in the Sahel a few years ago because it didn't rain for more than five years. And the area was difficult to reach with shipments of food from other countries.

In these times, however, there's more food available than ever, and a greater variety of food, as well. Clarence Cook, the living historian in the beginning of this book, said he didn't have corn flakes or peanut butter in his childhood. My own mother, who was born in Minnesota just a few years before Mr. Cook's birth in Chicago, often told us how she and her parents lived for weeks at a time on potatoes and "white gravy" made with flour and water. She carried lard sandwiches in her school lunch pail—bread-and-butter sandwiches with lard substituted for butter. In my depression-era child-hood an orange was a treat which we had only for Christmas. Yet in those  days orange-growers were burning them in huge piles because they couldn't sell them profitably. At the same time, the children of the Okies who came to California to be fruit-pickers were dying of vitamin-deficiency diseases that could have been cured by citrus products.

Poverty, not lack of food resources, is the problem. If there were fewer people, would more of them be rich?

Not likely. For the creation of wealth comes about, mainly, through providing goods and services to meet the needs and desires of the people. In Mr. Cook's "fastest century there's ever been" more and more products were developed because more and more people wanted or needed them.

Keeping food in a box on the back porch, as Mr. Cook's mother did, wasn't a very good way of preserving it. If it got too cold and froze and then thawed out again, it could spoil before it was cooked. Hanging containers of milk and butter into a deep well, as my mother did, provided necessary coolness but didn't do as good a job as modern refrigeration can. But without a large enough population to make the development of widely-available refrigeration profitable, would it ever have been done?

Being able to preserve food makes more of it available. One has to milk the cow or she'll go dry. But the milk will spoil quickly. Being able to transport food from where it's produced to where it's needed makes it available to more people. But without customers in sufficient numbers, who can afford to transport it? Being able to sell food or exchange it for other necessities encourages food-producers to grow more of it. So the concept of "fewer people—more food" simply doesn't work. That's not the way it is!

Mr. Cook had jelly sandwiches in his lunch pail. My mother didn't fare as well—hers were made with lard, no jelly. But neither of them mentioned throwing their sandwiches away. At a school in California recently the principal did a research study on food discarded by children in the school cafeteria. He found nutritious sandwiches containing meat, cheese and peanut butter still wrapped, untasted, and thrown out;

fruit with a bite or two removed; carrot sticks; half-filled milk cartons—all in quantities so astoundingly large that, if multiplied by the number of schools in the United States, the total would probably feed Bangladesh. But very few candy bars, snack cakes or cookies were tossed out. As the principal put it, "We didn't find any Twinkies in the trash."

Thirty percent of adult Americans are said to be overweight. We struggle with the consequences of over-consumption—obesity, heart trouble, hardening of the arteries and other health problems—while others suffer from having too little. We could live well on 2,500 calories a day. According to Barry Commoner, we produce 11,000 a day and eat 3,000-3,500. Much of the remainder is exported, but a significant amount is simply wasted.

I ONLY EAT 3500 CALORIES .... . PER MEAL ...... PLUS SNACKS....

Some of the concern over hunger is the result of exaggeration of the problem. We are still being told that two-thirds of the world's people go to bed hungry. Currently, one third of the population lives in the developed nations where the hunger problems are small, percentage-wise. So we would have to believe that virtually **all** of the people in China, India, Latin America and Africa go to bed hungry every night.

That two-thirds figure was a mistake made a quarter of a century ago by the U.N. Food and Agriculture Organization, and their correction of it never caught up, it seems. Lord Boyd-Orr, an agency director, assumed that anyone eating less than the 3,000-plus calories of the average European is malnourished, when in truth Europeans as well as Americans tend to be **over-nourished**, and many people get along nicely on half that much food.

What did you say, Billy? **You're** hungry? Maybe it's time for lunch.

Chapter Five.
Jumping to Conclusions

Want to play more games, Billy? How about jumping rope? That's a little young for you? Well, then, let's do high jumps or running broad jumps. We'll call it "Jumping to Conclusions."

Those who worry about how many people there will be have always been fascinated by numbers. Back in the late 1700s Thomas Malthus devised a system of projecting population by assuming that it grows by geometric progression (which it doesn't). By his system, doubling every 25 years, the world should have had, by now, something like 28 billion instead of the currently estimated four billion. The United States should have over half a billion and be approaching one billion less than a decade from now.

Paul Ehrlich, in his popular book *The Population Bomb*, declared that people grow at compound interest rates, the same way as money in the bank. They don't.

But because population levels are far below what mathematical formulas would have made them, explanations had to be found for the failure. So it was assumed that slow growth or no growth had been the normal state for human populations in the past, speeding up only about 300 years ago. Since **that** had to be explained, too, it was assumed that human populations always had high death rates, that our ancestors for thousands, perhaps millions, of years always died young.

That's the way the game is played, Billy. Take an idea and if it doesn't ring true, jump to conclusions to make it seem true. If by a certain theory the numbers should have been bigger, don't think about the possibility that the **theory** is wrong! Jumping to Conclusions is a very popular game!

JUMPING TO A CONCLUSION

Biological, cultural and historical facts do not support the conclusion that population was always slow-growing through high death rates in the past. Small populations merely struggling to stay alive don't build great cities, cathedrals, art galleries or castles. Such progress can only be achieved through some form of divided labor. Stone masons building a palace for the king weren't growing all of their own food or providing all of their other necessities. Others had to do that. Young men who served in the king's armies didn't grow their own food, either, or make their own armor, or manufacture their own weapons. For every person who had a specialized job—soldier, sailor, tinker, tailor, artist, musician, doctor—there had to be many others to provide necessary support (food, clothing, shelter, money, whatever it took).

Population growth undoubtedly enabled exploration for new lands that were needed. What men were building the ships? The same men who were tilling the soil? Not very likely!

In *The Great American Stork Market Crash*, I observed that Roman emperors occasionally took a census for tax purposes, and there's some fragmentary evidence of other population counts in other places, in other times. But periodic, definite, careful census-taking is a strictly modern development about 200 years old.

What evidence does exist suggests that large populations were not unknown in the past, and that people have been concerned about crowding in every period of history.

In the Bible, Genesis 13 refers to the carrying capacity of what is now Israel: ". . . The land was not able to carry them . . . and Abram said to Lot, '. . . Is not the whole land before you? . . . If you go to the left, I will go to the right, or if you go to the right, I will go to the left.' "

Euripides wrote that the Trojan War was due to "an insolent abundance of people." And many classical philosophers and historians such as Polybius, Plato and Tertullian worried about population growth, food shortages and environmental problems.

More recently, 180 years ago when Java was a Dutch colony with a population of four million, a colonial official complained that the island was "overcrowded with unemployed." Today Java is still thought to be overcrowded . . . and it contains most of Indonesia's 125 million people.

The following material is from my earlier book:

Justin Martyr, writing in the second century A.D., quotes Emperor Marcus Aurelius as saying his legions were surrounded by an army of nearly a million in Germany. That's a larger army than the Germans ever had again until the 20th century.

Josephus, in his accounts of the Jewish Wars, states that the census of Jerusalem taken by the priests for the Emperor Nero gave a Passover population of that city as 2,700,000. It included visitors, but only ritually purified Jews were counted; thus, it was not a complete count. Jerusalem today (1973—ed.) has 275,000 persons, and the entire country of Israel has 2,900,000— only 200,000 more than were counted in the city of Jerusalem nearly 2,000 years ago.

There's other evidence, too, that the world did not grow at a snail's pace during those early centuries. Archeological findings show that Yucatan, which today has five or six persons per square mile, had large cities, an advanced, civilized culture, and a great population density, a flourishing society thousands of years ago. Peru today has only 26 persons per square mile, but remains of cities have been found which are said to be as large as the early cities of Europe. Colombia is known to have had an advanced culture with large cities many thousands of years ago.

These are but a few examples. Much of the world which is barren or primitive today holds the remains of cities, cities built one on top of another. Vast civilizations have risen and fallen and risen again, century after century.

If our ancestors had been sickly and had therefore only a short life span, the human race would not have survived at all. Enough children had to survive to carry on the race; enough parents had to live to rear the children. Human beings are not like salmon; they do not simply spawn and die.

Historically and culturally, there had to have been a lot of people for civilization to develop as it did. Who built all those large cities the archeologists keep digging up? The Great Wall of China is

PROFESSOR!
I THINK I'VE FOUND SOMETHING!

VIDEO GAME CENTER

said to have required the labor of a million men. To have had that many working on a **single** job must have required a huge base population. And what of the pyramids, an astonishing engineering feat, built entirely by hand labor, as far as anyone knows? Small populations with a short life span certainly could not have done the tremendous things that have been done throughout the history of mankind.

If population students stopped considering growth in terms of mathematics and considered biology instead, it would be easy to see population growth (and decline) in reasonable concepts. Populations actually grow, level off or decline through **overreplacement, simple replacement** or **underreplacement** of the parental generation. There could have been—in fact, there must have been—periods of **normal** zero growth, times when generations were merely being replaced. Sustained high death rates among the young would have brought the human race to extinction. Sustained periods of underreplacement would have done the same thing. Many lost civilizations could have ended in just that way—by failing to replace themselves.

Cycles of growth makes sense; long periods of slow growth over millions of years do not.

Since the book was published, I've picked up other bits and pieces of evidence, too. Some I already knew, but hadn't mentioned before.

Those who believe that population growth was slow, barely moving, until about 300 years ago, attribute what they call "the population explosion" to the

impact of medical science. Yet it's been hardly over a century since Koch, Pasteur and others established the nature of infectious diseases and thereby laid the groundwork for fighting them. Surgery didn't become a great lifesaving technique until anesthesia and antiseptic methods had been developed—again, about a century ago. Dr. Edward Jenner discovered the process of immunization against smallpox less than two centuries ago, but it wasn't widely used until Pasteur's time.

Thus, if medical science really did the trick, why was it not claimed that rapid population growth didn't occur until between one and two centuries ago? The truth, of course, is that both historical events and the development of census-taking showed rapid growth occurring long before the medical profession came into great prominence.

The Council on Environmental Quality publishes a yearly report on the environment, including a chapter on population. In playing "Jumping to Conclusions" the council claimed that in America's early history people had large families but most of the children died. As one proof of this claim, they said that President Thomas Jefferson and his wife had six children but only two grew up. Well, President John Adams, who lived in the same era, was the father of five children, and they all survived. Which was more typical, the Jefferson family or the Adams family?

Modern medical researchers believe that Mrs. Jefferson had diabetes, a genetic disease which couldn't be controlled in those times. Her illness contributed to the deaths of four children in infancy. It also probably was the main factor in her own death some weeks after the birth of her sixth child.

High birth rates plus high **survivability** produce rapid population growth. And the United States grew very quickly in our first century. Census records show a doubling of the population four times between 1790 and 1890. Some of that growth came from immigration, of course, but more of it was the result of high fertility, average family sizes of seven or eight children. Large numbers of children may have died, but large numbers must have survived or we wouldn't have increased as much as we did.

Billy, did you ask how many times we doubled the population since 1890? This may surprise you, but it was only once. It was 63 million in 1890 and about 123 million in 1930. To double even one more time in our second hundred years we'd have to reach 246 million by 1990—seven years from now. Given our low fertility, it's not likely we'll do it. So contrary to what the population "experts" have been telling you, our "doubling times" are **not** getting closer and closer together.

Writing in the scientific journal *American Ethnologist* in February 1977, Michael Harner, an anthropology professor, offered evidence that the Aztec population in the valley of Mexico (where Mexico City is today) had grown to 25 million before Cortes and his soldiers ever arrived there. That's about twice as many people as live there now. He then jumped to the conclusion that the population was too large to be able to get enough protein from animal sources. Therefore they started the practice of human sacrifice and cannibalism.

But another professor, Ortiz de Montellano, has

refuted Harner's thesis in the following ways: (1) The amount of flesh available from sacrificial victims would not have provided much for the masses of people; (2) human flesh was reserved as a delicacy for the adult aristocrats; (3) only arms and legs were eaten—would truly hungry people have wasted the rest? and (4) times of human sacrifice coincided with the harvest—a time when food supplies would have been more plentiful rather than scarce.

ARMS?...
....'N'
I, LEGS ?
J.

Okay, Billy, maybe I shouldn't have included the human sacrifice story. It's unpleasant. But I needed it as part of the puzzle I'm trying to put together. If all the pieces could be found and reconstructed properly, it's possible one could show that (1) many populations were bigger in the past than they are today, and (2) commonly-held beliefs that large populations couldn't have been supported, and therefore, didn't exist, may not be true at all.

I had planned to end this chapter now, but I ran across another interesting bit that belongs here. Han Fei-Tzu, a Chinese philosopher who died in the year 233 B.C.—that's over 2200 years ago—was a population control advocate who believed that life "in the old days" was better when there were fewer people. He wrote that "nowadays people do not consider a family of five children to be large, and each child having again five children, before the death of the grandfather there may be 25 grandchildren." He jumped to the same conclusions that Paul Ehrlich did when he said that a couple with eight children would have 64 grandchildren for whom to buy Christmas and birthday presents! Family sizes simply don't stay the same and population growth doesn't continue at the same pace, indefinitely.

However, Han Fei-Tzu's remarks contain some interesting food for thought. He expected each of the five children to grow up and become parents themselves, and he also expected the father to be still alive when the 25 grandchildren were arriving. If most of the children born to a family commonly died and if the parents, as so many believe today, died young, why should Han have expected this, a grandfather not dying before 25 grandchildren were born?

A very large leap in the dark has been made by those who vastly over-estimate the reproductive ability of human beings. Charles Westoff, who writes frequently on population subjects, has said that if there were no forms of birth control, the average woman married 15 years would have 10.2 children. But natural sterility is a factor affecting 10 to 15 percent of all couples. Thus, to make up for the sterility of others, the family sizes of fertile women would have to be higher than 10.2 in order to produce that average number. If, for example, 15 out of every 100 couples were infertile, the average family size among the remainder would have to be 12 children. But there's also the problem of low fertility, couples who have difficulty conceiving even though they may not be actually sterile. Adding in that factor, the remaining couples would have to produce perhaps 13 or 14 children per family. There are literally dozens of other factors too complex to go into in a work of this type which would keep averages from being extremely high. Indeed, long before "planned parenthood" was ever a popular or possible concept, average family sizes were coming down.

Wayne Davis, the professor who is responsible for the idea of "Indian equivalents"—the oft-quoted view that a baby born in America puts 50 times more stress on the environment than a baby born in India—is another strong believer in the power of people to produce consistently high numbers of children. He bases his theory on the experience of the Hutterites, a small group of religious people living mainly in Canada and North Dakota. It is a precept of the Hutterite religion to have as many children as possible. Professor Davis gave 10.4 as the average, though later studies have indicated that the current average is nine (even for the Hutterites, the average has—and will—come down). But there's a big difference between setting out to have as many as possible and merely not trying to prevent having them.

Professor Davis says that the Hutterites' simple lifestyle keeps them healthy and, he says, they are hardly ever killed in automobile accidents or war. Therefore, the father of 10.4 children might live to see the arrivals of a few of his more than 11,000 great-great grandchildren. Davis, too, has made the mistake of assuming that average family sizes can and will stay the same, generation after generation, which they can't and don't.

OH, BOY....
11,000
BIRTHDAY
PRESENTS!

The Hutterite population, still very small, has doubled about four times in 100 years. Therefore, one could assume, with at least some degree of reasonableness, that the Malthusian concept of geometric progression (doubling every 25 years) could only occur if average family sizes were at least 10 children in every generation. But Malthus wasn't referring to family sizes that large. Never forget that he spoke of the **lowest** level of population growth.

What's that, Billy? I said I was going to end this chapter a couple of pages ago? I know. I do get carried away! Ah . . . Billy, do you mind? I just read something else that belongs in this chapter.

Some United Nations experts were commissioned to study population problems in 1970. They reported to U Thant, then Secretary-General, that population growth is difficult to measure since disasters of one kind or another have significantly altered population patterns in the past.

"Had there been no war, famine or epidemic since 1850," the commission reported, "the world's population might have totalled more than two billion in 1920."

They concluded, therefore, that enormous future increases in the numbers of mankind are "a virtual certainty" unless disasters "hitherto unimaginable" occur.

So what was the world's population in 1920? No one can say, for sure, but estimates range from just under two billion to over two billion! Thus the wars, famines and epidemics referred to had very little impact on population growth from 1850 to 1920. The arrival of the two-billionth person might have been delayed for five years, perhaps ten, but no more than that.

It shouldn't be so surprising. Prior to World War II, the victims of war were predominantly young men in battle. The girls who stayed home, plus the young men who didn't go, plus the young men who came back (not all of them died, after all) could keep the population going. For most of the boys killed in battle there were other boys to replace them in marriage.

Even in World War II, though bombings killed civilian populations as well as military, young men were still the primary victims. As long as there were—and are—women capable of child-bearing, and enough men to be fathers, the human race can continue. No war has yet destroyed **all** of the men; in addition, the ability to father a child isn't exclusively given only to the young. But women have definite limitations to their times of fertility.

Famine has not occurred on a worldwide scale. When it happens in a specific area, other people in other places are not affected. And where there is starvation, it is not the whole population which is starving. The most likely victims are the very old, who have already reproduced, and the very young. So long as there are enough young adults left to have more children, the population can continue. High infant mortality is tragic, but if the parents are alive, they can have another baby. Indeed, in more primitive times and more primitive places, breast-feeding is the usual mode of nourishing an infant. If the baby dies, he or she is often quickly replaced as the mother, now not nursing, is susceptible to pregnancy again. This is not to say that breast-feeding is **always** a deterrent to pregnancy, but it's a highly significant factor, especially when the nursing infant is not given other foods.

There have been no worldwide epidemics except the flu pandemic occurring during World War I. Other epidemics have been limited to smaller areas, and no disease has been known to wipe out an entire population, or even the largest part of the population, in modern times. With diseases, too, just as in the matter of malnutrition, the ones most likely to die are the very old and the very young, and preservation of the child-producing group can keep the population from dying out.

Possibly, there's another factor that hasn't been considered: Survival instinct leading to increased fertility. Within animal populations, this is known to exist. In Europe, for example, where concerted efforts have been made to wipe out foxes because of a rabies problem, female foxes now frequently have litters of eight to ten pups instead of the four or five that used to be more common.

It could be that war, famine, and pestilence have kept the human race going instead of cutting it down. For when "it's summertime and the livin' is easy" mankind may have a tendency to drift along. Malthus said—and this is the part of his thesis that rings true—that if ever there were a perfect form of birth control, the natural indolence (laziness) of man is such that the human race would never develop to its proper size.

I can't say that **my** conclusions are correct, in all respects, but I have as much right to jump to a conclusion as anyone else does! And much of what I'm saying offers, at least, a logical explanation of why the human race hasn't succumbed to the forces that were supposed to keep it down.

U Thant's commission's concern that "enormous future increases" are certain has failed to take into consideration that much of the world is headed in exactly the opposite direction: Their populations are either declining already or can be expected to decline in the decades ahead.

Hey, Billy, come back! I know this got to be a little heavy for you, and you lost interest. But wouldn't you like to hear about energy? Come on—that's the next chapter, and I promise this one has ended. Right here.

Chapter Six.
Population, Energy
And Resources

Billy, when my son Michael was your age, about 22 years ago, he thought he would never have a chance to drive a car. He was convinced from what he heard at school that we would run out of oil before he was old enough to have a driver's license. So, you see, the idea of running out of resources isn't a new worry, not something that's just come to the surface.

Many resources, however, were not recognized as important in other times. It's known that petroleum was an ingredient in the making of asphalt more than 6,000 years ago. It's been burned in lamps and stoves for a long time, too. It's had some real medicinal uses, plus some fake ones—it was the "snake oil" of the traveling medicine man. But it wasn't in extremely high demand until the invention of the automobile and development of the gasoline-powered engine.

Since petroleum is a fossil fuel, it's in the class of resources called "non-renewable." When we run out of it, there won't be any more. This will happen, sooner or later, no matter how many or how few people there are. A source of fuel will have to be found to replace it. Who says we can't find one—or a dozen, for that matter.

Natural gas, another fossil fuel we're always worried about running out of, was once considered to be

of so little value vast
quantities were simply
wasted. I've read that in
the 1930s a person could
walk across the state of
Louisiana at night and
have his way lighted by
gas which was being

burned off, deliberately (such gas was the unwanted
side effect of drilling for oil). Half a century ago only a
few million American households used natural gas for
cooking and heating. Now 56 percent of our homes are
burning it. Since it has become commercially valuable,
suppliers take pains not to waste it. And since the price
is going up, consumers are becoming conservation-
minded. Yes, we'll run out of it some day. But there are
other ways of producing burnable gas—from coal, for
example, or from garbage, sewage or trash.

Wood had become a common fuel for cooking and
heating in many countries in the past, and it's still the

GEORGE.... WE NEED
MORE FIREWOOD !

fuel of choice in lesser developed nations today. So there has been mounting concern that all the forests will be destroyed by hordes of people seeking firewood.

Depletion of forests has been a problem is some areas, but most nations have now learned how to avoid this problem. The forests in most areas are owned by someone—private individuals, corporations or governments—and people aren't free to chop them down at will. A few will illegally cut down a tree or two, but if large numbers were doing it, they would be stopped. Green wood doesn't burn well, anyway, and most firewood supplies picked up by non-owners come from fallen branches and dead trees.

Owners of the forest lands who cut the trees for profit from lumber, firewood or paper pulp generally replant. Wood is, therefore, a renewable resource, and forests are managed better today than they were a few generations ago when the infamous "robber barons" stripped them for fast profits with no thoughts of tomorrow.

In my childhood days we had neighbors who made their own electricity with a windmill. We used both wind and solar energy without realizing it when we hung laundry on clotheslines to be dried by the wind and sun. But there were some energy sources I never heard of then: Geothermal heat (steam from hot rocks deep in the earth) and nuclear power, both fission and fusion. Scientists at the University of Chicago were trying to smash atoms when I was your age, Billy, and I wish they hadn't succeeded in doing it. But they did, and since we can't put the genie back into the bottle, we'll have to concentrate on putting it to good use. Fusion, from what's been said and published about it, sounds quite safe and practical. Perhaps it really will be the answer to the world's hope for cheap, plentiful energy.

But our most important resource is the creativity of the human mind. Without it, even the best of raw materials cannot be fully developed; with it, even the poorest can be made useful.

Chapter Seven.
Button, Button . . .

Hey, Billy, I've devised a new game for you. Button, Button, Who's Got the **Panic** Button? The idea is to think up some wildly implausible happenings related to population—and make people believe them!

Paul Ehrlich said that if the growth rate continued at its present level (which he didn't know it couldn't) in 900 years there would be 60 trillion people on Earth. A British physicist, J.H. Fremlin, suggested that number could be housed in apartment buildings 2,000 stories high covering the entire face of the globe. But beyond that number growth could not continue because we would have reached a "heat limit" and the "world roof" would be hot enough to melt iron.

Another "panic button" story of Ehrlich's is how we "just missed" a population-destroying epidemic in 1967 when a crate of monkeys infected with a previously unknown virus were in the London airport en route to a laboratory in Marburg, Germany. Two weeks later seven of the 32 lab workers who contracted the disease had died of it. Ah, but if somehow the disease had broken out in the London airport, Ehrlich said, it could have spread around the world within a matter of hours (because travelers at the airport were heading for various countries). But I can't help wondering what

that incident had to do with the dangers of population growth. Wouldn't it be more likely that large populations would have a better chance to develop resistance than small ones would? Wouldn't it be more likely there'd be a lot of survivors? After all, 25 of the lab workers who fell sick did live.

Ehrlich's book is filled with "panic button" stories, but one of my favorites appeared in a speech he gave at the First National Congress of Population and Environment in 1970.

"We could be a single volcanic eruption away from the end of civilization," he said then. "A volcanic explosion equivalent to the explosion of Tambora in 1815 could wipe out agricultural production for a full year over much of the world."

So why didn't civilization come to an end in 1815?

Incidentally, there have been other volcanic **explosions** which affected the world's weather. But none of them put an end to civilization except at certain spots, such as the destruction of Pompeii in the year 79 A.D. by the eruption of Mount Vesuvius. When the island of Krakatoa blew up in 1883, the dust could be seen throughout the world. The weather is said to have been greatly changed. When Mount Pelée in the West Indies erupted in 1902 it disrupted the magnetic field in the atmosphere and, with it, the weather patterns. But the civilization of the world didn't come to an end.

Lester Brown (director of Worldwatch) panicked a lot of people in 1974 by announcing that there was only a 27-day supply of grain left to feed the whole world. I had a chance to challenge him on that at the World Population Conference in Bucharest later that year.

"That 27-day reserve is for feeding the total population of the world," I pointed out. "Under what circumstances would the entire population have to be fed out of its reserves? Only in total disaster, in which case it wouldn't be possible to distribute it, anyway." He conceded that the panic was unjustified, but claimed that when the supply falls below a 66-day level, the price goes up. That may well be true, but that's not the same as saying we don't have enough food.

Some "panic button" stories aren't so desperate, but might still be useful in the game. Ellen Peck, author of *The Baby Trap*, says that every time 35 children are born in the United States, we have to build a new classroom for them. That would be about 100,000 classrooms a year, give or take a few. But we're having almost a million **fewer** children a year and could well be closing the existing classrooms at the rate of 25,000 annually.

Ms. Peck's claim would be true only when there are **extra** children—more than those already attending school. That's what happened in our baby boom years, but it isn't happening now, and wasn't when she wrote her book in 1971.

Other "panic button" games are being played by those who worry that the genetic qualities of the human race are declining. (The "poor stock" is producing "too many" babies, they say; the "good stock" is having "too few.") They claim that medical science is keeping alive too many people with genetic defects and the "gene pool" is being "polluted." You know, Billy, I remember what happened the last time somebody who had a bit of power started talking about pollution of the gene pool. Fellow's name, I recall, was Adolph Hitler.

Then there's the "panic button" stuff about the "greenhouse" effect caused by emissions from factories,

Other "panic button" games
are played by those who
worry about the genetic
qualities of the human
race declining.

HAVE
ONE
BABY

HAVE
FIVE
BABIES

HAVE
12
BABIES

GO

BABIE

PANIC   A GAME FOR
ALL AGES

FERTILITY
CARD

heated buildings and such. I'm not quite sure whether that's supposed to heat the earth so that the icebergs melt, flooding coatal cities, or if it's supposed to cool everything enough to create a new ice age. Whichever, it's a potential disaster. But there were ice ages and big floods before human beings were building factories. Nature itself is pretty good at producing "greenhouse effects"—with exploding volcanoes, for example.

I'll give you a "panic button" story, myself, derived from a news item I ran across some time ago. It was headed "Old World Aging" and appeared in the *Kansas City Star*, April 13, 1977. The story explained how Great Britain had survived many wars and diseases, but what would finally kill her off would be "just plain old age." Because of her low birth rate Britain, like most other Western nations and the United States, is growing old. For Britain the population projection for the end of the century is a population 25 percent smaller than it is today, and it will be "an army of old-age pensioners supported by dwindling numbers of working-age people."

Suggestions were made for coping with the problem: Either admitting massive numbers of young workers from poorer countries or pushing up the retirement age to 80 or 90, or possibly both (immigration and late retirement). Read that again—that's a real panic button, that part about the retirement age. Eighty or 90 years—I swear to you that's what it said. People who are already 62 to 72 years old will be 80 or 90 by the end of the century. Raising the retirement age to that level would mean, in effect, virtually no retirement. Work until you drop dead.

In the United States there's serious talk of raising the retirement age to 68 or 70 in order to keep our Social

Security system afloat. But our fertility decline is as drastic as England's or as any other Western nation's. So perhaps that "68 or 70" will be revised to "78 or 80" before we know it. But one alternative being advocated is euthanasia to directly reduce the number of old people. How's that for panic? But not really implausible, is it?

I'd like to throw in one more panic button story. This one's a computer game. It's a take-off on what the Club of Rome (a group of industrialists and economics experts) did with computers to produce a report called "The Limits to Growth" which projected imminent disaster if growth didn't stop at once.

Later the same group produced a new report to correct the "obvious errors" in the first one. It was called "Strategy for Survival" and said that growth was needed. But it received almost no attention.

Since there are also limits to decline if the human race is to survive, my story is about what happens when you feed the computer with factors on decline rather than growth. It's plausible except that computers have not yet been developed with emotion. The story appears in *The Great American Stork Market Crash.*

The Club of Rome, Georgia, was composed of several prominent, educated persons who were

deeply concerned with the too-rapid downward plunge of the American birth rate. They included two obstetricians, four educators, three manufacturers of baby products, a biologist and several economists. They decided to conduct a computer project to find out what would happen and when to expect the worst.

A group of talented student researchers at Georgia Tech were assigned to the task. They gathered every available statistic to determine when the American people would cease to exist as a viable nation. They collected such items as the percentage of decline in the birth rate, the decline in marriage rates and the decline in the number of marriages that were lasting. They considered the rate of increase in sterilization operations, rising abortion rates, percentages of increased sterility due to venereal disease and related subjects. They computed the quality of life without children. They figured out the rates of economic decline in such fields as education, which were dependent upon a young population. They included the rate of decline in our defense establishment due to the shortage of young service personnel.

Finally, the big moment came when the computer was ready to spew out the fateful answers. Jerome Forrest, the supervisor of the project, found himself unable to watch. The sense of impending doom was too great. He went to his office, after first leaving word for someone to come and tell him the results.

He was just sitting at his desk, staring at a picture on the opposite wall, trying not to think, when a student researcher came in, a look of shock and horror clearly visible in his eyes.

"Professor Forrest," he stammered, "I—sir—I don't know—I can't tell you—"

"Go ahead, Tom. I know it's bad news. Just give it to me straight," Forrest said quietly.

"Yes, sir. Well, sir—" the student took a deep breath, gulped and made the announcement.

"Professor, the computer is **crying**."

Chapter Eight.
Population Patterns
And Profiles

Billy, do you have some building blocks? Not the little baby ones with alphabet letters on but any like the Lego kind that fits together like bricks. Let me have them and I'll show you the population profiles that illustrate growth, stabilization (true zero growth) and decline.

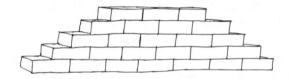

Note that when population is really growing the profile is a kind of pyramid, with the lower levels (the younger part of the population) always larger than the one above it. The ZPG profile has become rather straight-sided, with each generation nearly the same size and only the top layer being much smaller (due to

the dying-off from old age). A declining population is represented by an upside-down pyramid, with the younger age groups on the bottom and the older ones on top.

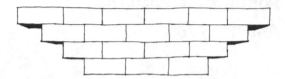

For much of our nation's history our age groups made pyramids, with each one being a little bigger on the lower levels and smaller at the top. In the late 1920s and the 1930s the pattern began to change, with a smaller group, because of the too-low birth rate, taking its place at the bottom. There are now more 50-year-olds than 40-year-olds in our population.

As World War II ended, the Baby Boom began, and once more our population profile seemed to be taking on a pyramidal look. But as the birth rate dropped in the late 1950s, we were approaching a zero growth pattern. We were just barely above the average family size that would result in each generation being nearly equal in numbers, the only way zero growth can happen normally, when Ehrlich wrote *The Population Bomb*. We didn't need any urging toward population stability—we already almost had it. But the panic started and the "stork market crash" was upon us. Now we're forming another new look in our age profile, the beginning of an upside-down pyramid.

On some of his Tonight Show appearances Dr. Ehrlich has talked about his concept of "instant cities." He says that the difference between the birth rate and the death rate gives us every year a potential city the size of Detroit. In reality, we are **subtracting** cities, for not enough children to make up a comparable population in the future are being born. The young adults who would be the core group of the same size nation in the future have not all been born. And, by the way, Detroit itself is declining at the rate which would subtract a Baltimore every ten years!

At the beginning of 1970 there were 58 million children under 15. Now there are only 51 million. Even more startling is the drop in the under-five age group. In 1970 there were 20 million of them; in 1980 there were only 16 million. We are subtracting Detroits quite rapidly.

In Clarence Cook's "fastest century" the cities

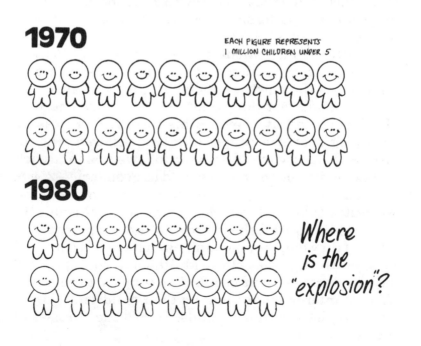

1970

EACH FIGURE REPRESENTS
1 MILLION CHILDREN UNDER 5

1980

Where is the "explosion"?

were growing. One of them, St. Louis, is now back to the population level it had in 1890, the year before Mr. Cook was born. Other cities which are steadily declining include Chicago, Philadelphia, Baltimore, Washington, Cleveland, San Francisco, Boston and many more.

The concept of "population explosion" was built on false methods of projecting population growth. I mentioned them earlier in this book—geometric progression and compound interest—now I'll try to explain them.

Thomas Malthus is the man who is usually credited with the idea that populations, unchecked by war, famine or pestilence, will grow geometrically, doubling every 25 years (presumably with each new generation). He further stated that this growth would occur—that is, in geometric patterns—even at the lowest level of increase possible.

Malthus had no historical evidence for his thesis. The only country which had begun to have a periodic census was the newly-established United States, and we had made just one count. There's only one way Malthus could have devised his theory. That was by assuming that if a couple had two children who, in turn, each had two children, who followed suit and each had two children, the result would be geometric—2, 4, 8, 16 and so on.

But it takes two people, one male, one female, to have a child, and brothers and sisters don't marry each other. If they did, they couldn't **each** have two children! To show the fallacies of the Malthusian concept, we'll have to start with four people (two couples) to show the effect of inter-marriage among their children.

Billy, let's cut paper dolls. Here's the first set of couples:

This is the first generation, two sets of parents. They can represent two million sets, or two billion, or whatever number you wish. The results will still be the same, as far as the theory is concerned.

Here are the children of the first generation. There are four of them, plus the four parents, so now there are eight. And this would be a doubling. But see what happens after that!

The second generation marries, and each new couple has two children. That's four, and the three generations added together now make 12, not 16. There is no doubling effect in the third generation. Each new couple now having, again, two children each, would make the total 16—4, 8, 12, 16. Not geometric. And by now the first generation would be dying off, in all likelihood, and each new generation would be no more than four. The population at this point would have ceased to grow.

Of course, in real life, as we've already seen, the two-child family would bring on population decline. This would happen even if every couple actually had two children, not as the top limit ("no more than") but as an average, and even if every child grew to adulthood. It takes more than two because there's an imbalance between boys and girls—always.

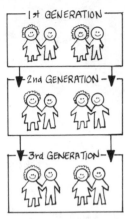

TOTAL: 12 PEOPLE

In real life, of course, not all children do survive, not all people do marry, not all couples do have children. Thus, it takes a mixture of sizes to obtain the needed average (on which there is some disagreement. Some demographers say 2.1, some say 2.2, most say 2.3).

Historically, many populations have doubled rapidly—for a time. Our own did it four times during our first 100-year post-census period (as previously noted). At first glance it would appear that Malthus was right. But remember that he said the doublings would occur at the **lowest level** of increase. We had large average family sizes in those days, plus immigration.

An interesting result of the Malthusian theory was the development by Charles Darwin of his "natural selection" or "survival of the fittest" thesis. Darwin didn't note the fallacy in Malthus' geometric progression, and he decided that with that kind of growth, the earth would be covered with elephants in a few thousand years. He concluded, therefore, that such growth was prevented because only the most fit of the species was able to survive.

Elephants, however, would have a tough time covering the earth, in any case. The female elephant doesn't begin reproducing at an early age—not early in relation to such animals as dogs and cats, for example. She is 14 or 15 years old before she reaches reproductive age, and the gestation period takes nearly two years. And like other mammals, she has a limited span of reproductive years.

Darwin's "natural selection" theory may have some validity, but if it does, it's for the wrong reason. He started with a false premise, so if he came up with

the right answer, it was purely accidental!

Paul Ehrlich (and other writers who echo his views) uses a compound interest method to project future growth. He takes the birth rate and the death rate of a given year, subtracts the latter from the former to get a "growth rate," assumes it to be a fixed one and projects it forward indefinitely.

A growth rate is useful in comparing this year's population with the year before, but it's not a tool for making projections. The rate is **not** a fixed one. Biologically it's impossible, for a fixed rate would have to be applied to everyone, to babies and children who are not yet reproducing, to women who are past child-bearing years and to men, who can't get pregnant, after all. Mathematically it's not possible, either, for the changing base also changes the rate.

Suppose I told you, "A baby was 20 inches long at birth. She was 30 inches tall at one year."

She had grown 50 percent taller in a year. It's possible, though unusual, that she could grow ten inches in her second year, but if she did, it would not be 50 percent, it would be 33 1/3 percent. If, however, you had continued to use 50 percent as your projection figure, you'd have to say that by the age of four she'd be more than eight feet tall! Since you never saw a four-year-old who was eight feet tall, you'd know there was something wrong with the projection method. With population the rates are so small the error is not so quickly seen. But the principle is exactly the same: The rate is not fixed; it is, in fact, determined by the **growth itself**, not vice versa.

It is only when the rate is set in advance that compounding it is possible. It works with money invested at a fixed rate of interest. People don't grow

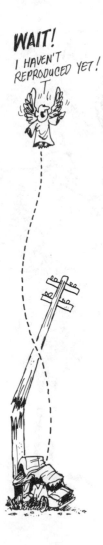

WAIT!
I HAVEN'T
REPRODUCED YET!

that way, and I'd venture to say that nothing else does.

Since everybody dies eventually, the death rate as a factor in population growth is not extremely important except when it's very high among the young (especially young adults who have not yet reproduced but whose parents are too old to have more children) or when it represents a very severe epidemic or other disaster. What matters is whether or not the person who died was replaced (or over replaced) within his or her own reproductive years.

The death rate in the United States is low at the present time, but as our population ages, it will rise. A worrisome figure has surfaced in recent Census Bureau reports, however. Although the overall death rate is still low, there has been an 11 percent rise in mortality in the 15-to-24-year-old age bracket, mainly because of accidents, homicides and suicides. It's a hidden "time bomb" really, for the effect on our age structure will be significant. Apparently, though, nobody's worrying about it but me!

To see the real picture of a nation's population future you cannot focus on the year-to-year birth and death rates. You have to know the fertility rate and the average family size in that generation which is now of reproductive age. In our Baby Boom years the average family size was about 50 percent higher than replacement size. That's why we had a spurt of growth. Today it's about 20 percent lower than required for replacement and is still falling. That's why decline, not growth, should be our concern for the future. But decline doesn't come suddenly, for the parents and grandparents are, in large numbers, still on the scene.

Chapter Nine.
Third Child Theme

Some population controllers aren't worried about actual numbers so much. They're simply convinced that small families are better than large ones. They like to produce studies that indicate that small families are brighter than large ones. But the studies have a hidden flaw, for it isn't valid to compare the first child in a two-child family with the fifth child in another family, for example. To determine the real effect of family size on intelligence one would have to compare the children within the same family with each other, not with children from other families.

To explain further, if a couple has two bright children, there's no reason to believe a third child born to that family would be less bright. Birth order—one's place in the family—undoubtedly has some effect on personality traits and development but not on raw intelligence.

Just for fun, I've been collecting information about third and later children who played important roles in history, music, art, literature and other aspects of civilization. Not that it proves anything, but many presidents were third or later children—Grover Cleveland (fifth of nine, in fact!), Andrew Jackson, William Henry Harrison, James Garfield, William McKinley (seventh of nine) and Zachary Taylor. And there was David, king of Israel—seventh according to some Bible verses, eighth according to others. There were military heroes from big families—Richard the Lion-Hearted (a third child, himself), Napoleon Bonaparte and the Duke of Wellington (who was Napoleon's nemesis at Waterloo). Among the musicians were Beethoven and the great pianist, Artur Rubenstein, who in his own words, "came late and unwanted to the Banquet of Life." He was a seventh child and his mother had planned to abort him.

John and Charles Wesley, the founders of Methodism, were members of a large family. Benjamin Franklin was said to be a 15th child. The Kennedys and the Rockefellers came from large families that have been highly successful. George Washington was the first child of his mother, but the sixth child of his father.

Among famous writers from large families were the English poet, Alfred Lord Tennyson, one of the Bronte sisters who was a third daughter, the American author Stephen Crane (best known for *The Red Badge of Courage*) and—surprise!—William Shakespeare, who was a third child.

The late Dr. Thomas Jermann, in one of his fine articles on population, suggested that it may be essential for human ecology that some people should come from large families and some should come from small ones. Dr. Herbert Ratner, editor of *Child And Family Magazine*, has pointed out that the interaction of siblings seems to be important to development. He believes that it's better for a child to have **both** a brother and a sister than to be part of a one-girl-one-boy family. Under ancient Jewish law a couple was supposed to reproduce until they had a boy and a girl. In reality, then, many families were quite large, for it wouldn't be unusual to have two or more girls before the arrival of a boy (or vice versa).

In an article called "Where Have All The Children Gone?" in *USA Today* (the journal of the Society for the Advancement of Education), Joseph McFalls, a sociology professor at Temple University, suggests that new technology will alter family sizes drastically. He explains that some techniques are being developed to ensure sex selection. So a couple who wants a boy and a girl will be able to achieve this kind of family in two pregnancies. Since a third child won't be needed to obtain the "right" sex, the number of births will decline.

Studies have indicated that twice as many women and three to four times as many men prefer male offspring over female (women's lib, where are you?). So, according to Professor McFalls, the new technology will produce a large imbalance of males over females. That, of course, will create a number of social problems.

He feels, however, that "the government will almost certainly intervene, probably by licensing the procedure to assure that equal numbers of boys and girls are selected."

Billy, maybe you were right—the turn of the century was a better time, but not for the reasons you gave. It must have been at least a time of greater personal freedom when the only kind of family-influencing certificate any governing agency ever thought about was a marriage license.

Conclusion. Survival And Other Games. "Too Many of Me"

I've heard that in schools there are games being played in classrooms to illustrate such things as population growth and human survival. One involves a lifeboat and the need to throw some people out in order to save the rest.

We played a similar game in my college days in sociology class at the University of Kansas. The idea was that some sort of disaster had made it impossible to save all but two out of a handful of potential survivors. There weren't enough supplies, you see, for more than that. We had to choose the two who would be allowed to live to rebuild the human race. I recall that one person was a poet, one a minister, one a farmer, one a scientist and the last a young boy (I'm sure there were others, too, but these are the ones I remember most clearly).

The poet was the first to be thrown out, which bothered me because, in those days, I fancied myself a poet! The minister had to go because the new race would make up its own religion in due time. The farmer got quite a few votes because he could grow food. In the end, the chosen two were the scientist and the young boy.

I had abstained from voting on the grounds that not enough information had been given, and now I wanted to know, "Is the scientist a woman of child-bearing age and how old is the young boy?"

The professor said he didn't know—that information had not been included in the game.

I was profoundly puzzled. "You're going to choose the people to restart the human race and you don't even know if you've got Adam and Eve?"

Another game I've heard about is one in which all of the students are jammed together into half of the classroom to illustrate how crowded it will be when the population doubles.

WE'VE GOT TO ENLARGE THE GYM!

This game was played at the high school where I was invited to lecture on population for the first time. My first talk was given in an auditorium where 1500 students had gathered. There was ample room, of course—this was a place designed for large gatherings. But for my second lecture I was taken to an ordinary classroom into which more than one hundred students had been placed.

My reaction was an involuntary gasp, "Gee, maybe there **has** been a population explosion, after all."

I quickly realized how the impression had been created, however.

Nowadays, with the school population falling so rapidly, a modern version of the game should be putting half the students into a room and sending the others out to the playground, out of sight. This would illustrate dramatically what happens in a declining population. At the present time, though, I haven't heard of anyone playing it this way. The emphasis seems still to be on population growth and crowding.

Sometimes there's an unconscious playing of the game, with astonishing results. Dr. Germaine Greer, a leader in the feminist movement in the Western world, was sent to India to promote family planning. Her goal was to persuade Indian families to have fewer children. But she noticed that when she spoke, the entire audience moved into one-half of the room, crowding together, leaving the other half of the room for her. And she said, "When I looked at these people, I knew perfectly well who there was too many of. There was too many of me."

All of those who speak of "too many people" have forgotten, it seems, to count themselves. And I throw out this challenge to them, "If you say there are too many, shouldn't **you** leave?"

But I don't want anyone to go before it's time. Everyone has a right to be here. My hope is that each of us will allow others the same right.

The one certainty about population growth is that each new addition is a little bitty squalling baby, a tiny scrap of humanity who hasn't made any problems yet for the world and hasn't had a chance to solve any.

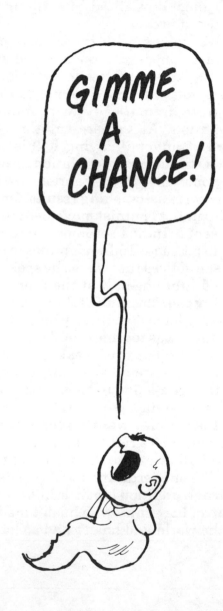

Chapter Notes

Because I find it too boring to make up bibliographies, I'm resorting instead to chapter notes which can be used to explain and identify sources of information. It's a method that also gives me a chance to include material I forgot about earlier!

Introduction
The story of Clarence Cook was adapted from information in a *Chicago Tribune* story reprinted in the *Kansas City Star*, Jan. 24, 1982, headlined "He didn't even have cornflakes."

Chapter One
I can't tell you the exact date of the *New York Times* ad which blamed pollution problems on the birth rate. I believe, however, it was printed in April, 1971.

Chapter Two
Most of the material in this chapter was included in my book, *The Great American Stork Market Crash*, Liguori Publications, 1973. Fred Domville's testimony was given in Washington in June, 1971.

Chapter Three
I know from past experience as a writer and lec-

turer that somebody is going to read this chapter and accuse me of wanting to fill every inch of the world with starving people just to motivate them to colonize other planets: That's not what I had in mind at all. I simply wanted to point out that what some imaginative writers have said is fundamentally true. Man's physical home, the earth, can survive only until the sun goes out. The sun is a star, and stars die.

The prediction of Charles Westoff on future U.S. growth and decline appeared in Planned Parenthood's journal. *Family Planning Perspectives*, reprinted in the *Kansas City Star*, April 16, 1978. Dr. Westoff conceded that in the long run, the decline must be halted. He said there would have to be considerable public investment in incentive programs to raise fertility. He suggested that the most useful one might be some sort of child care program that would permit women to work and have families at the same time. I found his new viewpoint—his vision of decline—rather amusing, for it's what I was telling him when I was a witness before the Commission on Population Growth and America's Future in June, 1971. (He was executive director of that Commission.) My argument then was that concern over women having "too many" babies was misplaced; our real problem was that they weren't having enough. He's the expert, but it took him seven years to see it!

He and other commission members expressed belief that fertility could be restored through a policy of paying for additional children. My argument then, and it's still the same, was that people don't have babies for money. That is, **most** people don't, and the few who would do so would not be sufficient to make a great deal of difference.

Dr. Westoff's projection of 250 million people before

decline begins is similiar to that of Campbell Gibson, chief of the Census Bureau. In an unpublished letter (Dec. 10, 1974) he said that an average family size of 1.8 plus the current level of immigration corresponds to the bureau's Series F projection and would, if continued, lead to a population size of 265 million in 50 years. It would then decline. He made some rough calculations at my request and concluded that the population in 200 years could be somewhere between 50 million and 100 million.

However, as I've suggested in this book, average family sizes don't stay the same, and it's more likely they'll be smaller rather than larger. So decline could happen far sooner than in 50 years, and the ultimate level of our population would then be lower.

Some reasons for continued family shrinkage were given in "Where Have All The Children Gone?" by Joseph A. McFalls, Jr. (*USA Today*, March, 1981). I summarize them here: High cost, the need for most women to work (75 percent of them already do, 90 percent may be doing so by the end of the century), unstable marital unions, late marriage, growing economic independence of women, changing attitudes toward women's roles, contraceptive use backed up by legal abortion, increasing acceptance of sterilization, new reproductive technology and increases in sexual deviation.

Economic incentives to increase child-bearing, as suggested by Dr. Westoff, are already being tried in a number of European countries. Cash grants, extended maternity leaves, loans for housing which are canceled if a couple has four children, family allowances only for those with three or more children—these and other ideas are being tried in both Western and Eastern

Europe, but without a great deal of success. In addition, most Eastern European countries have restricted their once liberal rules on abortion. Rumania, where the Pill, the IUD and surgical abortions are all now illegal, managed to double her birth rate—for one year. Now it's falling again.

When I was in Bucharest for the World Population Conference in 1974, I noticed that if I saw a couple with two children, one of the youngsters usually appeared to be about seven or eight and the other was an infant. I thought it was rather odd spacing, but I didn't know until later that Rumania had outlawed abortion in 1966 (after having liberalized it in the 1950s) and had banned most contraceptives in 1972.

Chapter Five

The account of Aztec sacrifices is adapted from a story in the *Kansas City Times*, May 8, 1978, headed "Aztec sacrifices not for food, study says."

The remarks of Han Fei-Tzu were adapted from *The Environment of America*, J.P. Ferguson Publishing Company, Chicago, 1971.

Professor Wayne Davis's projection of Hutterite population appeared in an article "Thoughts on Feeding the Hungry—More or Less People," June 20, 1970, and was distributed by ZPG chapters.

I'm sure that someone will come up with a computer model to challenge my remarks that one could assume, from the Hutterite experience, that it would take more than 10 children per family to double populations every 25 years. The model will probably show that it takes 5.8 or 6.1 or some such figure—I really can't say what number it would be, under ideal conditions. I'm only trying to say that **if** the Hutterite family size had been consistently over 10 and if the population doubled every 25 years (or four times in a century), perhaps a family size that large would be needed to continue such rapid growth. At least, the assumption would be **reasonable**, whether or not it was correct!

Quotations from the 1970 United Nations Population commission report appeared in the *Kansas City Star*, Nov. 19, 1972.

World Book Encyclopedia, 1939, quoted the Statistics Division of the League of Nations as estimating the world's population in 1920 at more than 1.7 billion, and the population in 1930 as "over two billion." A widely-distributed (though distorted) growth chart prepared for the World Population Society seemed to indicate 1920-1930 as the time when two billion had been reached. Many of the population control-oriented books published since 1950 have given the population of 1930 as either two billion or "over two billion."

The examples of large populations in times past are taken from Julian Simon's *The Ultimate Resource*, Princeton University Press. This is the best single book available for deeper study of the population issue.

Chapter Seven

I'd like to add more "panic button" stories and make additional comments on others.

On the matter of spectacular figures that can be achieved through assuming future growth at fixed rates, I loved the ones Fred Domville came up with in his testimony before the Commission on Population Growth (June 1971). He said, "The most breath-taking statistic I ever heard in my life came out of a Moody Bible Institute science film I saw in high school, and it was this: That if an ordinary microbe continued to multply at its normal rapid rate, **in five years it could fill all known space**. Beyond the farthest star, bllions and billions of light years away."

In his story of how we "just missed" a death-dealing epidemic in the Marburg monkey incident, Paul Ehrlich claimed that viruses grow stronger as they pass through large populations. Is this true? Not exactly. When a group of people are exposed to a **new** virus, they have little resistance and a high death rate can indeed result. **But** those who survive develop resistance and sometimes the ability to pass this resistance on to their descendants.

Ehrlich's only "evidence" that a virus could get stronger was the high death rate during the influenza pandemic as World War I was ending. But the affected population had gone through years of war and malnutrition which certainly must have lowered their resistance.

The Western World, particularly Europe, may have "just missed" dying off from another cause: Childbed fever. In his chilling book, *The Cry and the Covenant*, published in 1949, Morton Thompson told the story of how doctors themselves were spreading infection from one woman to another in hospital wards. In some places, virtually no mothers left the hospitals alive (and of course, the babies died, too). Fortunately for the general population of child-bearing women, most women did not go to hospitals or even have the services of doctors. Only the poor, the unmarried, the prostitutes, women who had nowhere to go and no one to care for them went to the hospital. Other women delivered in their own homes, generally with the help of midwives. It was, in fact, illegal at one time for doctors to deliver babies! The reason was that they were men and it just wasn't considered proper for men to attend women in such an intimate process as childbirth.

Dr. Ignatz Semmelweiss, the great man who discovered the cause of childbed fever, was born in 1818. He was his mother's fifth child. Her other children had been delivered by midwives, but it was now becoming a fad to have a doctor (even though at this time it was illegal to do so). The physicians who attended Mrs. Semmelweiss came directly from the university hospital, bringing with them on their unwashed hands and unwashed surgical clothing the germs of the dreaded illness. And Mrs. Semelweiss got it. However, since it was regarded as incurable, the doctors refused to come back to treat her—and she survived!

When little Ignatz grew up and became a doctor, he developed the theory that childbed fever was a contagious infection which doctors themselves were spreading from patient to patient without knowing it through their unwashed hands. Semmelweiss began using a strong carbolic acid solution for hand-washing and ordered all of the medical attendants on his ward to use it. His patients didn't get the childbed fever; the patients of other doctors did. In spite of his success, his theory was scoffed at by others, and it was at least 15 years before they were willing to accept it—15 years and thousands of deaths later.

Tragically, Semmelweiss died from the same disease—blood poisoning—that had killed so many mothers. He contracted the infection when he cut his hand while doing an autopsy on a woman who had died of childbed fever. It was the same year that Lister performed the first antiseptic surgery. Afterward, the medical world admitted that Semmelweiss had been right all along.

The saddest thing is that some in the medical profession believe it created a "populaton explosion" by saving lives and therefore the medical profession now has the right to "inhibit" the new life through abortion. Yet that same profession has been the **cause** of countless deaths among those who play the largest role in population growth, young women of child-bearing age.

Some might suggest that I've placed too much blame on doctors in the matter of childbed fever. Midwives didn't wash their hands, either. But the midwife, because she had to go from home to home rather than from bed to bed (as doctors did in hospitals) didn't have the same chance to pass on the **fresh** infection.

Chapter Eight

I mentioned, in this chapter, the rising death rate among 15 to 24-year-olds in the United States. I should add further information to the percentage quoted. That figure—an 11 percent increase—was for the period 1960 to 1978. From 1977 to 1978 it increased three percent. Obviously, it's advancing at a greater pace than before and should be cause for alarm.

It would be cause for even greater panic if those deaths were occurring predominantly among young women. No, I'm not exhibiting female chauvinism! I'm referring to the biological disaster resulting from the shortage of women capable of having children.

What could be called "the female factor" in population growth can't be emphasized strongly enough, yet it is so frequently overlooked by those who devise all kinds of theories about population control. In my earlier book, I asked the question, as a chapter heading, "Is The Population Bomb Female?" I'd like to include some parts of that chapter.

A movie script writer named Robert Ardrey became an anthropologist and wrote a number of books which gained acceptance for his theory that population control is the law of the species. He claimed that only man, with his religion and such, has strayed outside the bounds of this law.

As part of his thesis, he discusses the role of the "breeding territory" as a population-control device. Adam Watson of the University of Aberdeen carried out an experiment with red grouse on a moor in Scotland. He sought to prove that breeding territory actually eliminates healthy young adults from the breeding population.

Space for breeding was unlimited, but in the competition for territories not all were successful. Watson then cleared 119 territories by shooting or capturing the proprietors, that is, the male birds who had won the rights to them. Within a week, all of the territories were filled by new males from an apparent reserve breeding stock. Thus, Watson successfully demonstrated that it is the shortage of breeding territories that limits the breeding population.

But isn't it possible that it's the shortage of available females which keeps the extra males from being able to establish territories for themselves? Without a mate, a male's territory would be useless for procreative purposes.

Eliot Howard in 1920 demonstrated, through observation, that among countless species of birds the female is unresponsive to an unpropertied male. This, says Ardrey, keeps the disenfranchised male from breaking up any homes.

He himself studies the Uganda kob, an African antelope whose breeding pattern seemed to follow that of the birds, with territorial possession being necessary to attract females. Males fight for the territory, and the females will accept only the victorious males. The surplus of unsuccessful males, then, must amuse themselves in their bachelor herds. This type of behavior occurs also among some other antelope varieties, and Ardrey considers it a natural form of population control. But these animals live in herds, headed by a male, and he mates with more than one female. Therefore, the offspring may be as numerous as if each female had a separate mate. Ardrey has missed this important point: No matter whether a female has one mate or several, she still can produce only the number of offspring she is capable of producing. A bird can lay just so many eggs, whether she has one mate or ten; a human female can bear a child for only one man at a time.

It is the **availability of females**, rather than any behavioral, physiological or cultural patterns, which is the **key** to population growth. Primitive tribes may instinctively know what educated, civilized men seem not to know. That may be why, when they practice infanticide, it is the girl baby who is sacrificed. In a normal population, there are usually 105 or 106 boys for every 100 girls. In some primitive tribes, where infanticide is commonly practiced, the ratio may run as high as 150 boys to 100 girls. The males are "excess population," contributing nothing to **future** growth.

In most populations male births out-number female, and scientists have concluded that nature has to give males a head start in numbers because the females have greater survivability. But isn't it far more likely that the excess of males is a subtle kind of population control? From a strictly biological standpoint, nature wouldn't care whether or not every female had her own mate. One male could father any number of children; he is limited by the availability of potential mothers.

The tradition of our society to follow family lines descended from the male (it is the **father's** name which is carried on) tends to obscure the absolute importance of the woman's role in population growth.

The Mormon leader, Brigham Young, had 19 wives and 57 children. It would be easy to respond with "Wow! Think how big the population would be if every man followed his example!"

But every man **couldn't** follow his example. There would not be enough women to go around. And Young himself could not have fathered 57 children with only one wife. Had each of his wives had an **unshared** mate, a husband of her own, the total number of children might have been more than 57. Or it might have been less, for the inclusion of 18 other males would create a mulitiude of factors which would have affected the total.

I have referred to the fertility rate as "average family size," but more precisely, it's the "average number of children per woman." And it is the replacement of **daughters** that demographers (those who study population statistics and trends) are concerned about when they speak of "replacement fertility." The whole thrust of population theory would be altered if emphasis were placed upon women rather then men. Robert Ardrey, at least, would know what lies at the heart of a breeding territory!

Chapter Nine

Most of the information about people who were the third or later children in their families came from various volumes of *World Book Encyclopedia*. It isn't meant, of course, to be a **full** listing of famous third children. Such information is very difficult to dig out— often it simply isn't given.

Conclusion

The story about Dr. Germaine Greer was adapted from a newsletter printed by Alliance for Life (January 1982) and their story, in turn, had been adapted from an article by Erika Sanchez, staff writer for the *Dallas News*.

. . . And In Further Conclusion, Some Final Words

I know there are many who will demand more documentation of what I've said. "Where did you get that statistic?" is a common question from college audiences. All I can say is, "What kind of evidence did Thomas Malthus give?" Yet he went down in history with his false theory that's still being dredged up every few years and offered as the truth, the whole truth and nothing but the truth. The ghost of Malthus haunted the halls of the World Population Conference, with speaker after speaker using his concepts to prove how big the world will be if we don't establish population control.

A cartoon published in a daily newspaper at the conference drew a parallel between Count Dracula, the legendary Rumanian human vampire, and Malthus.

Many population control advocates make perfectly outrageous statements that should cancel out their images as "experts." When Paul Ehrlich wrote that the young of the human species goes through a long period of dependency because he is born with a small head and a small brain that grows and develops after birth, why he was still seen as so brillant? What other animals are born with full-sized heads and full-sized brains?

My number one all-time favorite "wild one" comes from a brochure printed by Planned Parenthood Federation (right from headquarters, too!): "Ten thousand years ago there were more lions than people in the world."

Just a flat statement, no source given. And in my mind's eye I could just see those census-takers sneaking around in the jungles trying to count those lions (and probably getting eaten in the process!). The people came out ahead, though, even when some of them (notably Christians) were being tossed to the lions as a "spectator sport" for Roman citizens.

Recommended
Resources

Readers who are new to the whole range of questions and activity surrounding population concern and the life issues may find the following list of organizations helpful. American Life Education and Research Trust recommends that every concerned American get involved with one of the groups described below, according to your interests and abilities.

Education

American Life Lobby (A.L.L.): The American Life Lobby is the largest grass-roots-based pro-life, pro-family organization in the world. Its educational resources include *ALL About Issues*, a monthly newsmagazine covering topics of concern to the pro-life movement. The Education Office boasts the widest supply of publications and materials available to pro-life, pro-family activists anywhere. Additionally, the Research Library contains original documentation, news clippings, research papers and historical data under hundreds of headings for ease of access by pro-life researchers.

A.L.L. State Advisory Committee (SAC): The State Advisory Committee is a vital information exchange with grass-roots members providing A.L.L. with newspaper clippings and reports on anti-life activities to the national office. In turn, A.L.L. sends out Alerts and Updates to keep SAC members totally up-to-date on legislation, government action and fast-breaking events of concern to our cause.

A.L.L. Chapter Association (A.L.L.-C.A.): A.L.L.'s Chapter Association program allows local and statewide groups to enjoy first priority access to the resources of the national office, personnel, materials and personalized assistance. Associated groups can also use the A.L.L. logo and name in connection with their local work, advancing mutual goals.

Write to: American Life Lobby, P.O. Box 490, Stafford, VA 22554.

American Life Education and Research Trust (ALERT): The American Life Education and Research Trust is breaking new ground in the publication and distribution of low-cost educational materials for use by local activists. Through ALERT, original research is being undertaken which will provide pro-life groups with accredited documentation needed to firmly establish key medical and statistical questions as they relate to abortion and related pro-life issues.

Write to: American Life Education and Research Trust, P.O. Box 279, Stafford, VA 22554.

Political Action

Life Amendment Political Action Committee (LAPAC): LAPAC is the oldest and largest of the pro-life political action committees, one which proved its effectiveness in the 1978, 1980 and 1982 elections. LAPAC not only provides funds directly to pro-life candidates, but undertakes extensive grass-roots education programs and coordinates local activities to elect pro-life candidates to federal elective office.

Write to: Life Amendment Political Action Committee, P.O. Box 1983, Garrisonville, VA 22463.

Clinic Activism

Pro-Life Action League (PLAL): The Pro-Life Action League has won national recognition for its full program of clinic activism ranging from curbside counselling, to picketing and demonstrations, to civil disobedience. Its efforts have directly saved many hundreds of babies and closed down several clinics. PLAL has also been instrumental in pushing for restrictive abortion regulations in a number of states and has gained much favorable publicity for the pro-life movement by working to educate and direct the media.

Write to: Pro-Life Action League, 6369 N. Lemai Avenue, Chicago, IL 60646.

Service and Counselling

Women Exploited By Abortion (WEBA): In less than one year Women Exploited has grown from two concerned individuals to over 10,000 women in 34 states. WEBA provides post-abortion counselling and group support to women suffering trauma and post-abortion psychological problems.

Write to: Women Exploited By Abortion, Lorijo Nerad, national coordinator, P.O. Box 267, Schoolcraft, MI 49087. (616) 679-4069.

Alternatives to Abortion International (AAI): Alternatives to Abortion International is the largest worldwide network to crisis pregnancy centers. AAI provides start-up materials, including training, for those beginning and operating crisis pregnancy centers and publishes *Heartbeat*, a magazine for counselors.

Write to: Alternatives to Abortion International, 46 N. Broadway, Yonkers, NY 10701.

Birthright: Birthright is a non-sectarian emergency pregnancy service offering positive alternatives to abortion. Birthright believes in the right of every woman to give birth to her child in dignity and the right of every child to be born.

Write to: Birthright, 686 N. Broad St., Woodbury, NJ 08096.

Christian Action Council Crisis Pregnancy Centers: The Crisis Pregnancy Centers are a locally organized and fronted ministry which provide alternatives to abortion for women with stress pregnancies. Through the CPC, care and practical help are made available to them. This ministry stands in total contrast to the commercialism of the abortion clinics that sell only the expedience of death.

Write to: Christian Action Council, 422 C Street, NE, Washington DC 20002.

Literature

American Life Education and Research Trust is concerned and active in the whole range of life and family issues. If you are new to questions of population and the value of human life, or if you simply want more information, the following books and monographs are highly recommended.

Handbook on Population, by Robert L. Sassone, Ph.D. This book is one of the author's several valuable reference compilations. Here the population alarmists find their claims refuted and their errant prophecies remembered. Facts and figures abound. $2, American Life Lobby, P.O. Box 490, Stafford, VA 22554.

Handbook on Euthanasia, by Robert L. Sassone, Ph.D. This volume examines and refutes all the euthanasia propaganda points, and in numbered paragraphs offers a reference guide for combatting the living will mentality. $2, American Life Lobby, P.O. 490, Stafford, VA 22554.

Secular Humanism, by Rev. Henry V. Sattler. Various streams of thought have merged to form the broad family of beliefs identified today as secular humanism. Dr. Sattler patiently deals with each slippery aspect of the modern phenomenon, showing its characteristics and its relationship to its historic roots. $3.95, Anastasia Books, P.O. Box 279, Stafford, VA 22554.

Know Your Body, by Charles Norris, M.D., and Jeanne Owen. Parents and young teens can read this little gem together to begin discussions of sexuality. It can be used in junior high or high school curricula and by adults as a primer for fertility awareness. $4.50, American Life Lobby, P.O. Box 490, Stafford, VA 22554.

Pro-Life Media Handbook, by Judie Brown. Defenders of life often feel they do not get good press, but the author says, "Good press comes from playing the game right, and by the rules." If you want to use your media opportunities intelligently, this book is the place to begin. $1.50, American Life Lobby, P.O. Box 490, Stafford, VA 22554.

How to Understand the Congress, by Robert G. Marshall. All your life you have been represented by a Congress, but you've never known what to do with it? Here is the owner's manual! This 40-page booklet will allow you to communicate effectively with your congressman and senators. $2, American Life Lobby, P.O. Box 490, Stafford, VA 22554.

Special Report on Global 2000, by Julian L. Simon. There is a mass movement to achieve environmental and population policy goals, using frightening but fallacious research to impress the gullible. Who embodies the movement, and what do they want? $1, American Life Lobby, P.O. Box 490, Stafford, VA 22554.

Infants at Risk, by Robert D'Agostino. The planned death of handicapped newborns is now commonplace and explicitly defended on "quality of life" grounds, while the authorities gaze blindly at the laws which could prevent infanticide. What does the law say? Professor D'Agostino explains. $1, American Life Lobby, P.O. Box 490, Stafford, VA 22554.

Prolonging Life and Withdrawing Treatment: Legal Issues, by Dennis J. Horan and Edward R. Grant. This handy reprint surveys the legal decisions that relate to the ever-growing agitation concerning the right to live and the "right to die," through 1982. $1, American Life Lobby, P.O. Box 490, Stafford, VA 22554.